God's
Keeping Power

an interactive journal

book eight

being with God series

God's Keeping Power

Graham Cooke

Brilliant Book House

Brilliant Book House
6391 Leisure Town Road
Vacaville, California 95687
USA
www.brilliantbookhouse.com

Requests for information regarding Graham's ministry should be addressed to:
Graham Cooke
Future Training Institute
6391 Leisure Town Road
Vacaville, California
USA
office@grahamcooke.com
www.grahamcooke.com

Unless otherwise indicated, all Scripture quotations are taken from The Holy Bible, New King James Version. Copyright © 1979, 1980, 1982 by Thomas Nelson, Inc.

ISBN 978-1-934771-05-1

dedication

This journal can only be dedicated to the Lord. He is the ultimate keeper. His love, generosity and kindness are the very foundation of our lives.

Unless we know Him as the One with power to save and keep us in the critical moments of life, we will never contend against the enemy, nor set foot on a battlefield where danger is present.

If we are to become more than conquerors we must be kept in a high place of confidence and faith.

acknowledgments

To my usual crew of Jordan, Tim and Carole without whose friendship and commitment to excellence this project would not have been so successful.

To all the people in my own life who are connected either to my family or the ministry, who have been so consistent and powerful in their love, prayer, wisdom, counsel and practical giving/support.

May God keep you as you have kept us. We owe you a debt of gratitude.

introduction

One person, with God, is always in the majority. This statement is foreign to our democratically-tuned minds, but it is true. One person, with God, has all of the power and authority. When things are tough, who would you rather be in friendship with? A thousand people who can't defeat one, or one who can defeat a thousand?

Who do you want standing next to you when everything goes pear-shaped? I want to stand next to my keeper – my best friend, the person who gave Himself for me, the one who wants me to succeed, the God whose joy it is for me to go further than I ever thought possible.

We cannot build a church without covenant friendships with God and man. We must drop the morality of the world and go for something deeper, better, and more profound in our relationships.

When we accept God as our keeper, we no longer have to pray, "Lord, come to me," because He will have discovered us to be a people who He can't stay away from. God cannot deny Himself. When He sees people living together in unity, He cannot stay away. Acts 1:14 tells us that the disciples were in *"one accord"* when the Holy Spirit blew into the Upper Room and changed the world. Everything in God longs to be amongst a people of one accord.

If we truly intend to rise up and be the Church God has called us to be, we will face persecution and opposition. God loves those hurdles. He loves to stand with us in the battlefield and be totally outnumbered. He laughs in the face of His enemies. "We'll just wait here," He tells the multitudes. "Why don't you go and get some reinforcements and come back. We'll still be here and we'll still beat you like an old drum."

One with God is always in the majority. It's a lesson of God's keeping power that we would be wise to learn.

Graham Cooke
March 2004

God's Keeping power

It was an ordinary evening in the wilderness for Jacob. The young man had spent the day traveling, as ancient nomads often did, before finding a place between Beersheba and Haran to camp for the night. Exhausted from his journey, Jacob fell asleep, using a large stone as a pillow.

This ordinary evening turned into an extraordinary experience with God. In his sleep, Jacob dreamed of a ladder between heaven and earth, with angels climbing up and down. At the very top, in heaven itself, Jacob could see the Lord standing. *"I am the LORD God of Abraham your father and the God of Isaac; the land on which you lie I will give to you and your descendants"* (Genesis 28:13), God told the young nomad. *"Behold, I am with you and will keep you wherever you go, and will bring you back to this land; for I will not leave you until I have done what I have spoken to you"* (Genesis 28:15).

Jacob awoke, stunned by what he had seen and heard. The Lord's words resounded in his ears: *"Behold,*

I am with you and will keep you wherever you go." The God who had created the universe had committed to being Jacob's keeper. Jacob couldn't believe how fortunate he was. *"Surely the LORD is in this place, and I did not know it,"* he said, shaking with holy fear. *"How awesome is this place! This is none other than the house of God, and this is the gate of heaven!"* God's glory, grace and loyalty awed Jacob.

> "A faithful friend is the medicine of life."
> Apocrypha

In return, Jacob took his stone pillow, set it up as a pillar, and anointed it with oil. He renamed the spot Bethel – "House of God" – and made his own vow back to the Lord. Jacob said:

> *If God will be with me, and keep me in this way that I am going, and give me bread to eat and clothing to put on, so that I come back to my father's house in peace, then the LORD shall be my God. And this stone which I have set as a pillar shall be God's house, and of all that You give me I will surely give a tenth to You.* (Genesis 28:20-22)

This power encounter changed Jacob's life. God kept him all the days of his life, turning him into the father of the tribes of Israel.

When God is our keeper, we can rest. We never have to fear or fret, we can confidently put everything into

His hands and trust Him. Understanding that God wants to keep us is a foundational principle of our spirituality. We must learn to rest in God's keeping power.

God doesn't slumber or sleep. He keeps us safe. He doesn't allow our foot to slip. He won't let you stumble. He never loses focus; He always pays attention. He protects us from the enemy, He keeps our soul safe. He guards us in every part of our journey.

Our rest flows out of our confidence in God and what He wants to be for us. When we worry, it's a sign that we don't fully trust God to keep us. Our low threshold of faith often takes us out of God's care because we think we have to do everything ourselves. We run all over creation trying to get help even though God Himself wants to keep us. He loves to protect us.

Instead of giving in to our soul – our mind, will and emotions – we must lean on His everlasting arms. The first place we should go when we're in trouble is the heart of God. When we live under that umbrella of His keeping power, we no longer have to pray for His presence to come. It's already with us.

> "To act the part of a true friend requires more conscientious feeling than to fill with credit and complacency any other station or capacity in social life."
> Sarah Ellis, British Missionary

We can have this same type of relationship with one another. Just as God has made a covenant to keep us, so we can be Christ-like in our friendships and keep others. All too often, Christians have Kleenex relationships, using a person once or twice and then throwing them away. This was not the model Jesus taught. It cuts Him deeply when men and women use and abuse one another. We are not called to look for reasons *not* to love each other.

ancient keepers

The principle of keeping and being kept had great significance in Israel throughout the Bible. It was an important principle for a man to ask someone else to be a keeper over his life and property. This idea was treated with reverence and care. Throughout Israel's history, one can read of keepers of the city gate, keepers of the king's forest, keepers of the house, keepers of the tabernacle, keepers of the door of entry, keepers of the sheep, keepers of the vineyard, and others.

Keepers were chosen for their courage, their integrity, and their skill. They were trustworthy individuals, proven in adversity. Keepers would not quit or back down in the face of opposition. They were incredibly loyal. A great keeper mirrored God's nature.

Because of the trust that flowed from a keeper being such a significant person, they were given responsibility for people and property that were very important or dear. It was a very personal thing to have a keeper.

David kept his father's sheep. Today, such a job sounds insignificant. But back then, livestock was a family's fortune and future. It represented all of Jesse's wealth. It was an honor for David to be trusted with the sheep. He defended them against raiders, bears, and lions. Before he went to enter his destiny in his unlikely victory over Goliath, Scripture records that he found another keeper to watch his father's sheep (1 Samuel 17:20). The scribe who recorded David's life knew that it was important to note how the future king cared for the things he was given to keep. David's subjects and descendants could be proud that even as a young man, he stood by his oath as a keeper.

> "Let me live in a house by the side of the road and be a friend to man."
> Sam Walter Foss

Being a keeper is not a casual thing. David didn't just grab the first bloke he saw and turn over his father's wealth to him. He searched for the strongest, bravest, most integrity-filled person he could find. "Would you come and keep my father's sheep while I am away?" he asked. The new keeper knew what an honor and responsibility it was to be asked to do this task.

Keepers can also be described as armorbearers. An armorbearer acted as a bodyguard, as someone who literally kept the head of his charge safe. It was the ultimate keeping responsibility, for a man's life hung in your care.

The lives of three men – Saul, Jonathan, and David – were irrevocably intertwined by keeping covenants. Jonathan had his own armorbearer while David served as Saul's. In the midst of those two relationships, a deep-keeping friendship emerged between Jonathan – the familial heir to Saul's throne – and David – God's chosen to inherit the throne. The challenges, victories and defeats these three leaders faced profoundly illustrates the power of a keeping covenant.

Jonathan and his armorbearer

In 1 Samuel 14:1–15, we read of one of Jonathan's mightiest exploits:

> *Now it happened one day that Jonathan the son of Saul said to the young man who bore his armor, "Come, let us go over to the Philistines' garrison that is on the other side." But he did not tell his father. And Saul was sitting in the outskirts of Gibeah under a pomegranate tree which is in Migron. The people who were with him were about six hundred men. Ahijah the son of Ahitub, Ichabod's brother, the son of Phinehas, the son of Eli, the LORD's priest in Shiloh, was wearing an ephod. But the people did not know that Jonathan had gone.*
>
> *Between the passes, by which Jonathan sought to go over to the Philistines' garrison, there was a sharp rock on one side and a sharp rock on the other side. And the name of one was Bozez, and the*

name of the other Seneh. The front of one faced northward opposite Michmash, and the other southward opposite Gibeah.

Then Jonathan said to the young man who bore his armor, "Come, let us go over to the garrison of these uncircumcised; it may be that the LORD will work for us. For nothing restrains the LORD from saving by many or by few."

So his armorbearer said to him, "Do all that is in your heart. Go then; here I am with you, according to your heart."

Then Jonathan said, "Very well, let us cross over to these men, and we will show ourselves to them. If they say thus to us, 'Wait until we come to you,' then we will stand still in our place and not go up to them. But if they say thus, 'Come up to us,' then we will go up. For the LORD has delivered them into our hand, and this will be a sign to us."

So both of them showed themselves to the garrison of the Philistines. And the Philistines said, "Look, the Hebrews are coming out of the holes where they have hidden." Then the men of the garrison called to Jonathan and his armorbearer, and said, "Come up to us, and we will show you something."

Jonathan said to his armorbearer, "Come up after me, for the LORD has delivered them into the hand of Israel." And Jonathan climbed up on his

*hands and knees with his armorbearer after him;
and they fell before Jonathan. And as he came after
him, his armorbearer killed them. That first
slaughter which Jonathan and his armorbearer
made was about twenty men within about half an
acre of land.*

*And there was trembling in the camp, in the
field, and among all the people. The garrison and
the raiders also trembled; and the earth quaked, so
that it was a very great trembling.*

Jonathan's armorbearer wasn't a junior caddy at the
local golf course. He was a mighty and respected
warrior who had been given the responsibility of
keeping the future king of Israel. As a
prince, Jonathan's keeper would have
been the second greatest soldier in the
land, behind only the man who kept his
father, Saul. This armorbearer was like
Jonathan's right hand; he didn't just
tote a bag of swords around. Time and
again, he put himself between Jonathan
and danger. He would have given his life for the prince.

> "A true friend unbosoms
> freely, advises justly, assists
> readily, adventures boldly,
> takes all patiently, defends
> courageously, and continues a
> friend unchangeably."
> William Penn

The level of trust between the two men ran deep.
Together, they secretly trekked toward the Philistine
garrison. But Jonathan knew that this armorbearer
wasn't his only keeper. He greatly trusted God's ability
to protect him and deliver a victory. *"Come, let us go*

over to the garrison of these uncircumcised; it may be that the Lord will work for us," Jonathan said. *"For nothing restrains the LORD from saving by many or by few."* The armorbearer didn't miss a beat: *"Do all that is in your heart. Go then; here I am with you, according to your heart." Let's do it,* **he said,** *I'm with you all the way.*

Jonathan was the kind of charge that could give a keeper a headache. He was a risk taker. He believed that God was more powerful than any force on earth. As his keeper, his armorbearer took all of the risks Jonathan wanted to take. Yet the keeper undeniably loved and trusted Jonathan: *"Do all that is in your heart."*

Jonathan hatched a quick strategy: "If they say, 'Stay where you are,' we'll wait for them. If they say, 'Come on up,' we'll go and kill them." At the same moment, both prince and armorbearer came out of hiding and showed themselves to the Philistines. They were ridiculed and taunted. "Come on up," one Philistine said venomously. "I want to show you something."

The duo had to climb up a steep crag to get to the Philistine garrison. Their hearts must have been pounding as they sensed what God was about to do. The armorbearer, carrying both his weaponry and Jonathan's, climbed on, showing that he was indeed a powerful man.

Jonathan stood up at the top of the rock and God moved. The Philistines fell at his feet. Together, Jonathan and his keeper killed twenty enemy soldiers straight away. In the distance, Saul and his advisors saw, heard, and felt the Philistines scattering. Stunned, Saul had to order a roll call to see who was missing. The victory became a famous one, and a rallying point for the dispirited Israelites. Men who had given up hope joined the fight as Saul, Jonathan and the Israelite army chased the Philistines.

> "For there is no friend like a sister in calm or stormy weather; to cheer one on the tedious way, to fetch one if one goes astray, to lift one if one totters down, to strengthen whilst one stands."
> Christina Rossetti

Jonathan's keeper fought the same battles as the prince. He was more than someone who carried a shield, he was a bodyguard and friend. He never quit, staying at even the riskiest moments. This was his call and his privilege as an armorbearer.

In a covenant relationship, the keeper must be willing to step out when a friend decides to take a leap of faith. *"Do all that is in your heart,"* the armorbearer said. When someone in a keeping relationship takes a risk, they don't do it alone; their friend goes too.

Saul and his armorbearer, David

While Jonathan's story is one of mutual respect and admiration, Saul's actions after choosing David as his armorbearer plunged his kingdom into civil war. Saul and David had a long, stormy relationship, but the king could not deny that the young man was loyal, powerful, and had significant integrity.

King Saul's life and empire was beginning to crumble. Having turned his back on God, Saul's life lost the protection of the Lord, who allowed an evil spirit to torment him. In 1 Samuel 16:14–23, we read of Saul's desperation:

But the Spirit of the LORD departed from Saul, and a distressing spirit from the LORD troubled him. And Saul's servants said to him, "Surely, a distressing spirit from God is troubling you. Let our master now command your servants, who are before you, to seek out a man who is a skillful player on the harp. And it shall be that he will play it with his hand when the distressing spirit from God is upon you, and you shall be well."

So Saul said to his servants, "Provide me now a man who can play well, and bring him to me."

Then one of the servants answered and said, "Look, I have seen a son of Jesse the Bethlehemite, who is skillful in playing, a mighty man of valor, a man of war, prudent in speech, and a handsome person; and the LORD is with him."

Therefore Saul sent messengers to Jesse, and said, "Send me your son David, who is with the sheep." And Jesse took a donkey loaded with bread, a skin of wine, and a young goat, and sent them by his son David to Saul. So David came to

Saul and stood before him. And he loved him greatly, and he became his armorbearer.

Then Saul sent to Jesse, saying, "Please let David stand before me, for he has found favor in my sight." And so it was, whenever the spirit from God was upon Saul, that David would take a harp and play it with his hand. Then Saul would become refreshed and well, and the distressing spirit would depart from him.

That's a tough gig for a worship leader: "I'm troubled by an evil spirit – come and play your guitar and get rid of it." David's humility and anointing led to Saul promoting him to one of the highest positions in the land: armorbearer to the king. He became Saul's keeper, going everywhere with him. He followed Saul into battle and would have sacrificed his life for him if necessary. The two had a covenantal relationship.

> "Your friend is that man who knows all about you, and still likes you."
> Elbert Hubbard

After playing his harp for Saul, David killed the Philistine giant Goliath. From that moment on, David lived with Saul and his family: *"Saul took him that day, and would not let him go home to his father's house anymore,"* records 1 Samuel 18:2. David's favor with Saul and the people grew rapidly. 1 Samuel 18:5 says: *"David went out wherever Saul sent him, and behaved wisely. And Saul set him over the men of war, and he was accepted in the sight of all the people and also in the sight of Saul's servants."*

This should have been a long and powerful friendship. David served Saul in good faith, while Saul envied David's rising star. In 1 Samuel 18:6–8, we read of the turning point in their keeping relationship:

Now it had happened as they were coming home, when David was returning from the slaughter of the Philistine, that the women had come out of all the cities of Israel, singing and dancing, to meet King Saul, with tambourines, with joy, and with musical instruments. So the women sang as they danced, and said:

"Saul has slain his thousands,
And David his ten thousands."

Then Saul was very angry, and the saying displeased him; and he said, "They have ascribed to David ten thousands, and to me they have ascribed only thousands. Now what more can he have but the kingdom?" So Saul eyed David from that day forward.

Saul's pride was wounded when the people celebrated David's victories. He forgot that when you have an armorbearer, the commitment flows two ways: it's a mutual thing in many respects. Saul remembered all of the promises David had made to him, but conveniently forgot the ones he had made to David.

From that day on, Saul set out to kill David. But because he had sworn to be Saul's keeper, David would not violate the armorbearing covenant.

> "The most I can do for my friend is simply be his friend."
> Henry David Thoreau

Saul didn't wait long to act. When the evil spirit came upon him the day after the "Saul has slain his thousands, and David his ten thousands" incident, David came to play his harp. This time, however, Saul had a spear: he threw it, yelling, *"I will pin David to the wall!"* David barely escaped.

These two men could not escape the vows they had made to each other. They were tied to each another spiritually because they were one another's keeper. Yet only David valued and understood the depth of this covenant, as we read in 1 Samuel 24:

> *Now it happened, when Saul had returned from following the Philistines, that it was told him, saying, "Take note! David is in the Wilderness of En Gedi."*
>
> *Then Saul took three thousand chosen men from all Israel, and went to seek David and his men on the Rocks of the Wild Goats. So he came to the sheepfolds by the road, where there was a cave; and Saul went in to attend to his needs. (David and his men were staying in the recesses of the cave.)*

Then the men of David said to him, "This is the day of which the LORD said to you, 'Behold, I will deliver your enemy into your hand, that you may do to him as it seems good to you.'" And David arose and secretly cut off a corner of Saul's robe.

Now it happened afterward that David's heart troubled him because he had cut Saul's robe. And he said to his men, "The LORD forbid that I should do this thing to my master, the LORD's anointed, to stretch out my hand against him, seeing he is the anointed of the LORD." So David restrained his servants with these words, and did not allow them to rise against Saul. And Saul got up from the cave and went on his way.

David also arose afterward, went out of the cave, and called out to Saul, saying, "My lord the king!" And when Saul looked behind him, David stooped with his face to the earth, and bowed down. And David said to Saul: "Why do you listen to the words of men who say, 'Indeed David seeks your harm'? Look, this day your eyes have seen that the LORD delivered you today into my hand in the cave, and someone urged me to kill you. But my eye spared you, and I said, 'I will not stretch out my hand against my lord, for he is the LORD's anointed.' Moreover, my father, see! Yes, see the corner of your robe in my hand! For in that I cut off the corner of your robe, and did not kill you, know and see that there is neither evil nor rebellion in my hand, and I have not sinned against you. Yet you hunt my life to take it. Let the Lord judge between you and me, and let the Lord avenge me on you. But my hand shall not be against you. As the proverb of the ancients says, 'Wickedness proceeds from the wicked.' But my hand shall not be against you. After whom has the king of Israel come out? Whom do you pursue? A dead dog? A flea? Therefore let the Lord be judge, and judge between you and me, and see and plead my case, and deliver me out of your hand."

So it was, when David had finished speaking these words to Saul, that Saul said, "Is this your voice, my son David?" And Saul lifted up his voice and wept.

Then he said to David: "You are more righteous than I; for you have rewarded me with good, whereas I have rewarded you with evil. And you have shown this day how you have dealt well with me; for when the Lord delivered me into your hand, you did not kill me. For if a man finds his enemy, will he let him get away safely? Therefore may the Lord reward you with good for what you have done to me this day. And now I know indeed that you shall surely be king, and that the kingdom of Israel shall be established in your hand. Therefore swear now to me by the Lord that you will not cut off my

descendants after me, and that you will not destroy
my name from my father's house."

So David swore to Saul. And Saul went home,
but David and his men went up to the stronghold.

This story is an interesting look into a keeping covenant gone awry. In an effort to protect his throne, Saul was out hunting his former armorbearer, David. Saul had forgotten the vows the two had made to each other, and now wanted to kill the man.

> "In a friend, you find a second self."
> Isabelle Norton

In the midst of their long war, God tested David's ability to keep his vows. Saul entered a cave, by himself, where David and his men were hiding. "This is your chance, Dave," the restless warriors whispered. "God has delivered Saul into your hands. Kill him." David crept towards Saul with his knife in his hand. The fighting, the running, the grief – it could all be over with one swipe of the blade.

Those few moments must have seemed like a lifetime to David. His mind must have been full of memories of he and Saul, laughing, planning strategy. He may have pictured Saul's face the day he killed Goliath. David also probably thought of his best friend Jonathan, Saul's son. He may have thought of his wife Michal and the day Saul gave her to be married to him. *I am this man's keeper*, David thought, *I can't kill him. If I kill him, I've killed myself, my best friend, my wife, and my country.*

David's knife flashed out and cut a patch of Saul's cloak. The men watching the scene probably groaned. "What is he doing?" they may have whispered. "Kill him!" David went back to the group and calmed them. *"The LORD forbid that I should do this thing to my master, the LORD's anointed, to stretch out my hand against him, seeing he is the anointed of the LORD,"* he said, restraining his men from taking matters into their own hands.

After Saul returned to his army, David sat for quite some time, turning the piece of cloth over and over in his hands. His conscience bothered him, Scripture says. Even cutting Saul's robe violated the keeping covenant he had made those many years before. While his friends – men who had left everything they loved to help David – said he would have been justified in killing Saul, David was grieved he had even cut his robe.

"The most persuasion of a friend is a strong thing."
Homer

David understood the power of a covenant. I think, at that point, he realized that he had lifted his hand against God's anointed, however innocently. Perhaps he felt as though God would take the kingdom away from him for his rebellion. Saul didn't even know anything had happened, but David was brokenhearted. He knew what he had to do in order to make this right. David ran out of the cave, calling Saul's name. The king stopped, turned, and watched in shock as his former armorbearer laid down, face first, before him. David, who moments before had the power to take Saul's life and kingdom, was now completely vulnerable before the man.

Saul listened as David confessed his sin, and showed him the piece of cloth. Looking at his sliced robe, the king realized what could have happened in that cave. "You're a better man than I," Saul said, shaken. "I know now that you will be king."

David could not kill Saul because, in his heart, he was still his keeper. It didn't matter what Saul had done or threatened to do. It didn't matter that Saul's heart was filled with aggression, hatred, violence, anger, and bitterness. David's vow wasn't contingent on Saul's behavior; it was about who David was. David had all of the justification he needed but he didn't use it. Even a small thing like cutting Saul's robe bothered him enough to throw himself on the mercy of God. That act of humility may have redeemed his own right to rule Israel.

> "A real friend is one who walks in when the rest of the world walks out."
> Walter Winchell

Where did David learn to honor his covenants? From his days keeping his father's sheep, and from his best friend, Jonathan.

Jonathan and David's keeping friendship

Fuelling Saul's jealousy of David was the fact that Saul's own son, Jonathan, loved David more than anyone else. Jonathan was David's keeper from the day he killed Goliath. 1 Samuel 18:1, 3–4 says:

> *Now when he had finished speaking to Saul, the soul of Jonathan was knit to the soul of David, and Jonathan loved him as his own soul ... Then Jonathan and David made a covenant, because he loved him as his own soul. And Jonathan took off the robe that was on him and gave it to David, with his armor, even to his sword and his bow and his belt.*

Do we love our friends as much as, or even more than, we love ourselves? With all of our heart, we should want the answer to be yes. Our friends must be as important to us as we are. Jonathan and David had their souls knit together. In other words, to unravel their friendship, one would have had to unravel his own soul. Keeping relationships can only be dissolved at severe damage to oneself. To back away from a dear friend is to cause ourselves harm.

Jonathan gave David the most precious gifts he had: his robe, his armor, his sword, and his belt. These gifts were both symbolic and functional. They symbolized

Jonathan's status as the heir to the Israelite throne. They spoke of his strength, his power, his might, his position. Jonathan knew that David was anointed by God to rule Israel; by giving the sheep keeper his armor, he indicated that he accepted God's choice. Saul wanted to build a royal line around Jonathan, but the prince wanted God's man, his best friend, to rule.

> "The difficulty is not that great to die for a friend, the hard part is finding a friend worth dying for."
> Henry Home

Jonathan's love for David didn't exclude Saul; it was the king who chose to step out of that pact. David was Saul's keeper, and Jonathan was David's. Father and son also shared a strong bond. Yet Saul's bitterness and pride kept fracturing what could have been an anointed, focused, powerful trio.

The prince did everything he could do to find reconciliation between Saul and David. In 1 Samuel 19:1–7, we read of one such effort:

> *Now Saul spoke to Jonathan his son and to all his servants, that they should kill David; but Jonathan, Saul's son, delighted greatly in David. So Jonathan told David, saying, "My father Saul seeks to kill you. Therefore please be on your guard until morning, and stay in a secret place and hide. And I will go out and stand beside my father in the field where you are, and I will speak with my father about you. Then what I observe, I will tell you."*

Thus Jonathan spoke well of David to Saul his father, and said to him, "Let not the king sin against his servant, against David, because he has not sinned against you, and because his works have been very good toward you. For he took his life in his hands and killed the Philistine, and the LORD brought about a great deliverance for all Israel. You saw it and rejoiced. Why then will you sin against innocent blood, to kill David without a cause?"

So Saul heeded the voice of Jonathan, and Saul swore, "As the LORD lives, he shall not be killed." Then Jonathan called David, and Jonathan told him all these things. So Jonathan brought David to Saul, and he was in his presence as in times past.

Jonathan loved both those men, and longed for them to be restored. In private, the son reminded the king of the good David had done. *"Why then will you sin against innocent blood, to kill David without a cause?"* he asked. Jonathan's words pricked Saul's heart, and the king swore he would spare David. The two reconciled, and things returned to normal for a period of time. Saul's rage, however, ran deeper than anyone could have imagined, and soon David was in danger again. As his anger increased, however, so did the covenant between David and Jonathan. In 1 Samuel 20, we read of how deep their bond had grown:

Then David fled from Naioth in Ramah, and went and said to Jonathan, "What have I done? What is my iniquity, and what is my sin before your father, that he seeks my life?"

So Jonathan said to him, "By no means! You shall not die! Indeed, my father will do nothing either great or small without first telling me. And why should my father hide this thing from me? It is not so!"

Then David took an oath again, and said, "Your father certainly knows that I have found favor in your eyes, and he has said, 'Do not let Jonathan know this, lest he be grieved.' But truly, as the LORD lives and as your soul lives, there is but a step between me and death."

So Jonathan said to David, "Whatever you yourself desire, I will do it for you."

And David said to Jonathan, "Indeed tomorrow is the New Moon, and I should not fail to sit with the king to eat. But let me go, that I may hide in the field until the third day at evening. If your father misses me at all, then say, 'David earnestly asked permission of me that he might run over to Bethlehem, his city, for there is a yearly sacrifice there for all the family.' If he says thus: 'It is well,' your servant will be safe. But if he is very angry, be sure that evil is determined by him. Therefore you shall deal kindly with your servant, for you have brought your servant into a covenant of the LORD with you. Nevertheless, if there is iniquity in me, kill me yourself, for why should you bring me to your father?"

But Jonathan said, "Far be it from you! For if I knew certainly that evil was determined by my father to come upon you, then would I not tell you?"

Then David said to Jonathan, "Who will tell me, or what if your father answers you roughly?"

And Jonathan said to David, "Come, let us go out into the field." So both of them went out into the field. Then Jonathan said to David: "The LORD God of Israel is witness! When I have sounded out my father sometime tomorrow, or the third day, and indeed there is good toward David, and I do not send to you and tell you, may the LORD do so and much more to Jonathan. But if it pleases my father to do you evil, then I will report it to you and send you away, that you may go in safety. And the LORD be with you as He has been with my father. And you shall not only show me the kindness of the LORD while I still live, that I may not die; but you shall not cut off your kindness from my house forever, no, not when the LORD has cut off every one of the enemies of David from the face of the earth." So Jonathan made a covenant with the house of David, saying, "Let the LORD require it at the hand of David's enemies."

Now Jonathan again caused David to vow, because he loved him; for he loved him as he loved his own soul. Then Jonathan said to David, "Tomorrow is the New Moon; and you will be missed, because your seat will be empty. And when you have stayed three days, go down quickly and come to the place where you hid on the day of the deed; and remain by the stone Ezel. Then I will shoot three arrows to the side, as though I shot at a target; and there I will send a lad, saying, 'Go, find the arrows.' If I expressly say to the lad, 'Look, the arrows are on this side of you; get them and come' – then, as the Lord lives, there is safety for you and no harm. But if I say thus to the young man, 'Look, the arrows are beyond you' – go your way, for the Lord has sent you away. And as for the matter which you and I have spoken of, indeed the Lord be between you and me forever."

Then David hid in the field. And when the New Moon had come, the king sat down to eat the feast. Now the king sat on his seat, as at other times, on a seat by the wall. And Jonathan arose, and Abner sat by Saul's side, but David's place was empty. Nevertheless Saul did not say anything that day, for he thought, "Something has happened to him; he is unclean, surely he is unclean."

And it happened the next day, the second day of the month, that David's place was empty. And Saul said to Jonathan his son, "Why has the son of Jesse not come to eat, either yesterday or today?"

So Jonathan answered Saul, "David earnestly asked permission of me to go to Bethlehem. And he said, 'Please let me go, for our family has a sacrifice in the city, and my brother has commanded me to be there. And now, if I have found favor in your eyes, please let me get away and see my brothers.' Therefore he has not come to the king's table."

Then Saul's anger was aroused against Jonathan, and he said to him, "You son of a perverse, rebellious woman! Do I not know that you have chosen the son of Jesse to your own shame and to the shame of your mother's nakedness? For as long as the son of Jesse lives on the earth, you shall not be established, nor your kingdom. Now therefore, send and bring him to me, for he shall surely die."

And Jonathan answered Saul his father, and said to him, "Why should he be killed? What has he done?" Then Saul cast a spear at him to kill him, by which Jonathan knew that it was determined by his father to kill David.

So Jonathan arose from the table in fierce anger, and ate no food the second day of the month, for he was grieved for David, because his father had treated him shamefully.

And so it was, in the morning, that Jonathan went out into the field at the time appointed with David, and a little lad was with him. Then he said to his lad, "Now run, find the arrows which I shoot." As the lad ran, he shot an arrow beyond him. When the lad had come to the place where the arrow was which Jonathan had shot, Jonathan cried out after the lad and said, "Is not the arrow beyond you?" And Jonathan cried out after the lad, "Make haste, hurry, do not delay!" So Jonathan's lad gathered up the arrows and came back to his master. But the lad did not know anything. Only Jonathan and David knew of the matter. Then Jonathan gave his weapons to his lad, and said to him, "Go, carry them to the city."

As soon as the lad had gone, David arose from a place toward the south, fell on his face to the ground, and bowed down three times. And they kissed one another; and they wept together, but David more so. Then Jonathan said to David, "Go in peace, since we have both sworn in the name of the LORD, saying, 'May the LORD be between you and me, and between your descendants and my descendants, forever.' " So he arose and departed, and Jonathan went into the city.

Just as Jonathan's armorbearer had told him to do whatever was in his heart, so Jonathan told David,

"Whatever you yourself desire, I will do it for you." In every covenant relationship, there are times when your friendship is tested severely. The promises and vows we have made to each other will be tested first. Our yes must be yes, and our no must be no.

David needed reassurance of where he and Jonathan stood because of Jonathan's love for his dad. Saul was trying to find David. David had to know if he could trust his best friend. Are you still my keeper, Jonathan?

> "My best friend is the one who brings out the best in me."
> Henry Ford

The two worked out a system to discover if Saul still wanted to kill David. Knowing how paranoid Saul had become, they created a signal to send the message in an innocent manner. Jonathan was now working against his own family and keeping his promise to David. David, thinking of his love for his own father, continually gave Jonathan a way out. "I don't want to put you in a difficult position, Johnny," he said. "This is your father we're talking about." But Jonathan didn't step out of his covenant. In fact, he increased it even further: "And as for the matter which you and I have spoken of, indeed the Lord be between you and me forever."

Can you imagine the cost of that to Jonathan? He wasn't just caught in the middle of a battle between his best friend and father, he was giving up his right to be king. He made the decision based solely on the fact that he was David's keeper. "When push comes to shove, I'm going to keep my word no matter what the cost is to me personally," Jonathan said. This covenantal relationship is real Christianity. Anything less than this is false, a substandard copy of what spirituality really is. Anything less than this depth of love and loyalty is the exact opposite of glorifying God. It dishonors Him and represents His Kingdom as far less than it truly is.

Saul was incensed. *"You son of a perverse, rebellious woman!"* he bellowed. *"Do I not know that you have chosen the son of Jesse to your own shame and to the shame of your mother's nakedness? For as long as the son of Jesse lives on the earth, you shall not be established, nor your kingdom."* Jonathan understood that we discover God in friendship, and that when we hold fast to one another in the most difficult circumstances, it glorifies Him. It is after the fire of passing a test of friendship that the presence of God resides among us.

Saul broke his covenant with David. Jonathan kept his at his own expense. He gave his place to his best friend, humbling himself completely. David became more important to Jonathan than his own life. In David's lowest moments, Jonathan encouraged him to persevere. 1 Samuel 23:16–18 says:

> *Then Jonathan, Saul's son, arose and went to David in the woods and strengthened his hand in*

God. And he said to him, 'Do not fear, for the hand of Saul my father shall not find you. You shall be king over Israel, and I shall be next to you. Even my father Saul knows that.' So the two of them made a covenant before the LORD. *And David stayed in the woods, and Jonathan went to his own house.*

Years later, when David heard of how Saul and Jonathan had been killed on the battlefield, he wept bitterly. His two keepers had been in danger, and he could not save them. Once David had been installed as king of all Israel, he remembered his vow to Jonathan, and adopted Jonathan's lone surviving son as his own. His commitment to keeping Saul and Jonathan's household extended even beyond death.

> "It is in the character of very few men to honor without envy a friend who has prospered."
> Aeschylus

a foundation for keeping

Keeping begins with our own relationship with God. The Lord is our greatest keeper, and the basis of all covenant friendships. If we can just grasp how the Holy Spirit promotes the keeping power of Almighty God in our lives, we will never be anxious or fearful again. God can be wonderfully trusted with everything: this is the foundation for a keeping friendship. He is our keeper, and He takes that role very seriously.

Once we understand that God is our keeper, we can begin to keep someone else. As He is, so we are. We must learn the dimensions of how God keeps us, and what He wants to be for us. God has places He wants to take us; He has a role in the Kingdom that only we can fill. God wants to commit each of us to outrageous adventures that, without Him, would scare the life out of us. With Him, it's fun!

Christians are not ordinary people: we are extraordinary men and women who do extraordinary things. With God as our keeper, we can be strong. When we don't understand God's keeping power, we stay in our little boats, too terrified to walk on water. Without God, we hide and wait for the battle around us to end.

> "The dearest friend on earth is a mere shadow compared to Jesus Christ."
> Oswald Chambers

But if we really believe God's keeping power, we can leap out of the boat and walk an entire sea with Him. We can become like Joshua, who asked God to freeze time so the Israelites could finish off their enemies. "I want to beat these guys," we can pray, and God will hold the sun in the sky. Earth lost a day because God kept His promise to a man. We are condemned to victory because God is our keeper. Psalm 121 testifies of God's keeping covenant:

I will lift up my eyes to the hills –
From whence comes my help?

My help comes from the LORD,
Who made heaven and earth.

He will not allow your foot to be moved;
He who keeps you will not slumber.
Behold, He who keeps Israel
Shall neither slumber nor sleep.

The LORD is your keeper;
The LORD is your shade at your right hand.
The sun shall not strike you by day,
Nor the moon by night.

The LORD shall preserve you from all evil;
He shall preserve your soul.
The LORD shall preserve your going out and your
*   coming in*
From this time forth, and even forevermore.

David's respect for keeping is well-illustrated in this psalm. He could call the Lord his keeper, because he knew what it meant. David had survived the murderous threats and attacks of Saul, the man he once bore armor for. He had spared that man's life because of his own vow to keep him. He had been delivered from certain death by Jonathan, his best friend and keeper. *"The LORD is your keeper,"* David sang, knowing full well the depth of such a relationship. *"The LORD is your shade at your right hand. The sun shall not strike you by day, nor the moon by night."* All of David's friendships were enriched because he knew that God was his most important keeper.

We must step into that place. Instead of living miserably and constantly worrying about what God is up to, we must step into the confidence and boldness which comes when we know that God is our keeper. He is for each and every one of us. What, specifically, does God want to

> "Friendship is a sheltering tree."
> Samuel Taylor Coleridge

be for you? Nothing is impossible once we discover His nature. As Isaiah prophesied,

> *"No weapon formed against you shall prosper,*
> *And every tongue which rises against you in*
>   *judgment*
> *You shall condemn.*
> *This is the heritage of the servants of the LORD,*
> *And their righteousness is from Me,"*
> *Says the LORD.*   (Isaiah 54:17–18)

A keeping God will always lead us to victory. The victory may be manifested in different ways. It may be through ultimate victory over our enemy. It could be in the realization of a promise fulfilled, faith proving out, a test passed with flying colours.

It can also be revealed in just holding on to God in the storm. At times there is a victory in learning to

stand when everything in you screams to run. Some of
my own victories have resulted in being the last man
standing after protracted warfare situations. Ultimate
victory is always connected with God's will being done
in the way that He desires.

As the Church, we are so worried about being
prideful or seeming overly triumphant that we back
down from talking about winning. We just don't
understand that the majesty, sovereignty, and power of
God will keep us and propel us into victory. Our lives
have been anointed for breakthrough, and God takes
His promises to us seriously.

In John 17:7–23, we read more of Jesus'
commitment to keeping each of us:

> *Now they have known that all things which You
> have given Me are from You. For I have given to
> them the words which You have given Me; and they
> have received them, and have known surely that I
> came forth from You; and they have believed that
> You sent Me.*
>
> *I pray for them. I do not pray for the world but
> for those whom You have given Me, for they are
> Yours. And all Mine are Yours, and Yours are
> Mine, and I am glorified in them. Now I am no
> longer in the world, but these are in the world,
> and I come to You. Holy Father, keep through
> Your name those whom You have given Me, that*

they may be one as We are. While I was with them in the world, I kept them in Your name. Those whom You gave Me I have kept; and none of them is lost except the son of perdition, that the Scripture might be fulfilled. But now I come to You, and these things I speak in the world, that they may have My joy fulfilled in themselves. I have given them Your word; and the world has hated them because they are not of the world, just as I am not of the world. I do not pray that You should take them out of the world, but that You should keep them from the evil one. They are not of the world, just as I am not of the world. Sanctify them by Your truth. Your word is truth. As You sent Me into the world, I also have sent them into the world. And for their sakes I sanctify Myself, that they also may be sanctified by the truth.

I do not pray for these alone, but also for those who will believe in Me through their word; that they all may be one, as You, Father, are in Me, and I in You; that they also may be one in Us, that the world may believe that You sent Me. And the glory which You gave Me I have given them, that they may be one just as We are one: I in them, and You in Me; that they may be made perfect in one, and that the world may know that You have sent Me, and have loved them as You have loved Me.

Jesus' prayer is littered with references to God's keeping power: *"Holy Father, keep through Your name those whom You have given Me,"* is but one example of His commitment to the idea. The same principle we saw unfold in the lives of Saul, David, and Jonathan, was brought into the early Church by Christ Himself.

> "When we know that He is with us, and for us, we have faith He will act on our behalf."

How does God want to be our keeper in our current circumstances? This is the beginning of faith for us. When we know that He is with us, and for us, we have faith He will act on our behalf. What could happen in our lives or ministries if we allowed God to exercise His authority as our keeper?

keeping as a covenant

After meditating on God's role as our keeper, we can then move on to pondering our commitment as a keeper of others. Who are the people we are called to keep? We need to pray, seeking God for those who He has given to us.

The temptation for Christians is to pick the people in leadership and volunteer to keep them, but a covenant relationship cannot be built on emotional blackmail. We cannot choose people based on our own soulish ambition to be connected with significant people in places of power, wealth or influence.

It is important to check our motives before the Holy Spirit. There has to be a genuine friendship involved. A love that is mutual; a trust that is present, however small.

Who are your friends? Are you called to increase your commitment to them?

In friendship, we can have defined relationships or assumed ones. To be a keeper, we must define the friendship. "This is what I want to be for you," we need to say. "This is what I need you to be for me." We must talk out our relationships, speaking out commitment, boundaries, and expectations, and come to an agreement on the way the relationship should unfold. Our success as a Christian depends on the quality of our relationship with God and the quality of our friendship with each other. Those two friendships must be knit together.

A keeping relationship is a covenantal pact between God and man, and between two people. Keepers have decided to intentionally bless another person in every way possible. The fruit of being kept is peace, as Isaiah prophesied in Isaiah 26:3 – *"You will keep him in perfect peace, whose mind is stayed on You, because he trusts in You."*

I believe that each of us needs to have our own keeping promise from God; something specific that we can hold on to. My own is found in Isaiah 42:6:

I, the LORD, have called you in righteousness,
And will hold Your hand;
I will keep You and give You as a covenant to the
people,
As a light to the Gentiles.

God gave me this promise almost twenty-five years ago, and I'm still living in the blessing of it. I still quote it, pray it, meditate on it. The Father has repeated these words to me over and over again. In the midst of conflict, warfare, difficulty, loneliness, criticism and persecution, this verse has come back to me.

> "No person is your friend who demands your silence, or denies your right to grow."
> Alice Walker

I have lost count of the many times people have come to me during an event or meeting and shoved a piece of paper in my hand. Almost eighty per cent of the time, the Scripture included is Isaiah 42:6. Why does God do this? Because it's my keeping promise. "Son, I'm your keeper," He says. "Don't forget that I'm the one holding your hand, supporting you and keeping you. I'm here for you, Grae."

A keeping blessing is a profound thing to hold on to, because it is a covenant. In Numbers 6:22–27, we read of one such blessing:

And the LORD spoke to Moses, saying: "Speak to Aaron and his sons, saying, 'This is the way you shall bless the children of Israel. Say to them:

"The LORD bless you and keep you;
The LORD make His face shine upon you,
And be gracious to you;
The LORD lift up His countenance upon you,
And give you peace." '

So they shall put My name on the children of
Israel, and I will bless them."

This was a keeping promise to the nation of Israel. No matter what they faced, this blessing would bring them back to focusing on God's name. "Use this blessing to invoke My name," God essentially said. Within this blessing, they had the right to call for help. It became a common banner under which all of Israel could stand, and it all flowed out of the Lord committing to be the nation's keeper.

When God keeps us, His face shines upon us. His blessings and grace surround us. He lifts up His face to us and gives us peace. God will do everything in His power to keep us. He wants us to succeed and be happy. His heart has been turned toward us.

> "A true friend is one soul in two bodies."
> Aristotle

vigilance in keeping relationships

The term "armorbearer" literally means "keeper of my head." It's interesting to ponder that our heads staying on our shoulders might be directly reliant on our best friend. This ups the ante of relationship. Keeping friendships include the concepts of helping, guarding, watching over, giving shade, and protecting. We must be constantly vigilant when we keep one another; our concentration must never waver.

For the people I've been given to keep, this idea of vigilance translates into thinking and praying for them. I look into their lives and ponder what is coming next. What's the Lord saying? How can I stand with them? Are they in trouble? Do they need my help? Do they need me to stand up? A keeper doesn't wait to be asked; he or she sees the danger and steps in. We talk with one another openly and honestly: "What is it you need from me right now?" To be vigilant, I must be willing to give away everything I have, down to my last penny.

Keeping is not a passive thing – it is active and serious. We must run our eyes over one another's lives. If my friend is attacked, I am being attacked. I want to go and stand with them. In the same manner that I know God keeps me, I want to keep them, offering a safe place for them to rest and have peace.

> "A true friend never gets in your way unless you happen to be going down."
> Arnold H. Glasgow

Vigilance is not only necessary in protecting one another from external pressures. We must also work against the pressure that builds within every relationship. When we commit to keeping someone, our word must be our bond. We cannot let go of it. As the pressure builds between a keeper and his or her friend, it becomes easy to step back from all that has been promised. Saul did exactly that with David, his armorbearer. David, however, took the more difficult route of honoring every commitment to the king. We must not cheapen our covenants.

Relationships come under fire all the time. There is a constant barrage of adversity and challenge that covenantal friendships must endure. It is in those moments that God either stands with us, and we with Him, or we lose a piece of the Kingdom. Our unity must not be diminished, for God loves to dwell with people who are in one accord. To have God's presence in our midst, we must face the day of testing first. If we put things ahead of people, we have failed. If we run away from our covenants, we have moved away from God. If we place our anointing or ministry or reputation ahead of one another, we have fallen to the wrong side of God. Vigilance in relationship must become our trademark as a Christian community.

upgrade your relationships

Every relationship goes through changes. No relationship stays at the same level continuously. Indeed every significant relationship must be re-invented every 3–5 years as a minimum. It will obviously depend upon the events and circumstances surrounding the friendship.

My relationship with Heather has gone through many stages where we have had to upgrade our covenant and learn how to be something different for one another. From girlfriend to fiancé, to young wife (lots of adjustments there!), from young mother to mother with school age children, then being parents of teenagers (we survived!), from being a wife and mother who earned a degree at university, who then had a full-time teaching post as well as a busy family – our love was tested and upgraded. In that period my own ministry was becoming more international. Someday my wife will be sleeping next to a grandfather (possibly the ultimate adjustment!).

At every stage of change we must take care to upgrade our covenants and re-invent our relationships. Relationships break down when people forget to progress their love to new levels of commitment, generosity and understanding.

Think about the people you have lost out of your life. How many of them could you still be involved with and enjoying a deeper friendship with?

Obviously some relationships are seasonal and others longer term. Defining relationships through loving dialogue enables us to determine what type of friendship we want to generate together.

Without definition we can only assume. It is our

assumption of what we mean to one another that often leads to the most damaging breakups. One person assumes that their friendship is at a higher level of commitment than another and then is grievously wounded when love is not returned at the same depth.

It may seem cold and detached to dialogue about where we are in our own friendship with someone. However, this type of conversation underpins the reality of love and actually makes our commitment more accessible.

Take time to redefine current friendships and reinvent your covenants with the people whom God has given to you. It gives your friendships a solidity and an energy that is powerful and transforming. Our actions follow our words, fleshing out our covenants in a way that releases life and expectation.

I know what I can expect from my real friends when my own life comes under threat. I know what I can contribute when they are in need. We can deliberately enjoy and endure good and bad times together, safe in the knowledge that we can celebrate our success and be lovingly held in our defeats. This is kingdom life and it enriches all who observe it.

transferring a keeping covenant

Situations do arise that call for one's authority as a keeper to be transferred to another. David, on his way to battle Goliath, found another keeper to watch his father's sheep. Jesus, on the cross, looked at His best friend, and transferred the responsibility of keeping His mother to him:

> *When Jesus therefore saw His mother, and the disciple whom He loved standing by, He said to His mother, "Woman, behold your son!" Then He said to the disciple, "Behold your mother!" And from that hour that disciple took her to his own home.*
>
> (John 19:26–27)

When my daughter, Sophie, moved to Tulsa, Oklahoma, for ten months, I went with her to do a conference in the church. During my visit, I took some of the men in leadership aside and asked them to look out for her. "I am her father," I told them. "I have kept her all the days of her life. But now she's coming to you for ten months and this keeping power needs to be transferred from me to you. I need you to take this seriously; she is the light of my life." These father figures formally accepted the responsibility of keeping Sophie for those ten months, promising to watch out for her, pray for her, and stand with her.

After her time in Tulsa, Sophie told me she felt completely at home. "Dad, it was just like being at

"A true friend is someone who thinks that you are a good egg even though he knows you are slightly cracked."
Bernard Meltzer

home," she said. "I could talk to them in the same way I talk to you. I knew I would have favor with them just as I have favor with you." Transferring a keeping covenant is something to take very seriously.

other scriptural keepers

In the New Testament, there may be no stronger keeping relationship than the one between Barnabas and Paul. Paul, then known as Saul, had been persecuting the church for months. He had even been present at the stoning of one of Christ's most devoted followers, Stephen. Saul would wreck homes, interrupt meetings, drag Christians off to prison, and was merciless in his persecution.

On his way to hunt down Christians in Damascus, Saul had an incredible conversion experience. He was healed of both physical and spiritual blindness and began preaching the same gospel he had once tried to snuff out. Naturally, the early Church was more than a little wary of Saul. Had he really changed? Or was he simply trying to infiltrate and dismantle the leadership structure?

Only one Christian was bold enough to take a chance on Saul. Barnabas, whose nickname was "Son of Encouragement," made the effort. Acts 9:26–27 records the story:

And when Saul had come to Jerusalem, he tried to join the disciples; but they were all afraid of him, and did not believe that he was a disciple. But Barnabas took him and brought him to the apostles. And he declared to them how he had seen the Lord on the road, and that He had spoken to him, and how he had preached boldly at Damascus in the name of Jesus.

Barnabas laid his reputation on the line for Saul. The two formed a unique partnership and began traveling together.

In the beginning of their joint ministry, we read of the adventures of "Barnabas and Saul." Barnabas was clearly the mentor; he helped, blessed, taught, supported, and encouraged Saul. The two worked for a year in Antioch, where *"they assembled with the church and taught a great many people,"* Acts 11:26 says. Even the Holy Spirit referred to the duo as Barnabas and Saul: *"As they ministered to the Lord and fasted, the Holy Spirit said, 'Now separate to Me Barnabas and Saul for the work to which I have called them'"* (Acts 13:2).

> "A friend loves at all times, and a brother is born for adversity."
> Proverbs 17:17

Yet Saul kept growing in anointing and authority. Eventually, he was renamed Paul to reflect how far he had come from his days of persecuting the church. Barnabas recognized Paul's anointing and served his friend's ministry. It was a complete reversal of roles. By the end of Acts 13, the two were referred to as Paul and Barnabas. What a wonderful picture of what real friendships are about.

In friendship, there are seasons when we put our friends first because it is their time to shine. We want to serve that call. And there are times when it tips the other way, and our friends are called to serve us. When we have committed to keeping one another, we can trust that we are out for each other's good.

Because Paul had seen, first-hand, the power of his keeping covenants with God and Barnabas, he was able to keep, in turn, young pastors and preachers like Silas, Titus, and Timothy. He said in 2 Timothy 1:12–14:

> "A man who has friends must himself be friendly. But there is a friend who sticks closer than a brother."
> Proverbs 18:24

> . . . *I know whom I have believed and am persuaded that He is able to keep what I have committed to Him until that Day. Hold fast the pattern of sound words which you have heard from me, in faith and love which are in Christ Jesus. That good thing which was committed to you, keep by the Holy Spirit who dwells in us.*

Paul wanted Timothy to hold on to the treasure which had been entrusted to him by God. *"Guard what was committed to your trust,"* he instructed in 1 Timothy

6:20. This is the crux of a keeping relationship: we want our friends to walk in the fullness of God's blessing for them. Even in the difficult times, our friends must be encouraged to hold fast to God: *"Therefore let those who suffer according to the will of God commit their souls to Him in doing good, as to a faithful Creator,"* Peter wrote in 1 Peter 4:19.

The epistle writers explored the issue of God's keeping power again and again. Jude touched on it in Jude 24–25:

> *Now to Him who is able to keep you from stumbling,*
> *And to present you faultless*
> *Before the presence of His glory with exceeding joy,*
> *To God our Savior,*
> *Who alone is wise,*
> *Be glory and majesty,*
> *Dominion and power,*
> *Both now and forever. Amen.*

God can keep us from stumbling, but only when we follow Jude 21's advice to *"keep* [ourselves] *in the love of God."*

"Faithful are the wounds of a friend."
Proverbs 27:6

Having God as our keeper, and keeping ourselves in His love, allows us to maintain a high level of spirituality. God is deadly serious about keeping.

The third strand of this spirituality is to keep a friend as well, as we read in Philippians 2:3–8:

> *Let nothing be done through selfish ambition or conceit, but in lowliness of mind let each esteem others better than himself. Let each of you look out not only for his own interests, but also for the interests of others.*
>
> *Let this mind be in you which was also in Christ Jesus, who, being in the form of God, did not consider it robbery to be equal with God, but made Himself of no reputation, taking the form of a bondservant, and coming in the likeness of men. And being found in appearance as a man, He humbled Himself and became obedient to the point of death, even the death of the cross.*

Can we allow our friends to change, evolve, and even surpass us in anointing and favor? Can we support them wholeheartedly? This is the test many of us will face again and again.

my keepers

One of my great friends, Tony Morton, has taught me more about grace than any human being alive. I love Tony. It is vitally important to me that Tony be at peace, and that everything he puts his hand to flourishes. If it's a choice between me doing well and him doing well, I would step back because he is more important. If there was just one blessing on earth and he and I stood there, I would want him to have it. Of course, I'd have to wrestle him to give it away, as he would be fighting to give it to me. We love each other and want to see the other succeed. His success is more important than my success. I am his keeper, and he is mine: I'll do whatever I can to see him prosper.

I have been blessed to have a number of keepers in my life, and a number of people who I keep. You do not have to talk through the keeping principles over and over; you just have to make a start with someone. The friendship and covenant deepens over time.

My personal assistant, Carole, has been with me since 1980. Carole and her husband, Alan, have been our friends and closest supporters in all that time, even moving cities and churches to remain with us. Periodically we talk abut the future and continuing together in ministry. We invest in one another's families in a variety of ways. These two always face spiritual warfare because of the call on my life. To be a keeper is a costly thing. When you walk with Jesus, you partake of all of the warfare He provokes.

> "Ointment and perfume delight the heart, and the sweetness of a man's friend gives delight by hearty counsel."
> Proverbs 27:9

I am very conscious of the warfare my friends face; that's why I take keeping them so seriously. I want to be responsible for who Carole is, and for the peace in her life. Alan prays for me, stays up at night for me, fasts for me. He will go into battle at the drop of a hat.

David and Marie have been my keepers for twenty-one years. They offer advice and support into our marriage. Heather and I can talk to them about anything. They keep our confidence, pray for us, give us wisdom, and help us sort things out. We see them regularly; we love them.

John and Christine have been in my life for many years. They are good friends and excellent prayer warriors They are keepers. They would fight for me, stand with me, contend against the enemy for me and give me support and encouragement. I know that I could call them from across the world and they would go into battle on my behalf. For my part, I have been their mentor and friend, training, supporting and creating opportunities for them to grow in their identity, destiny and calling.

Joy has been one of Heather's keepers for a long time. They chat together and pray for one another. Joy would defend Heather to the death; they're best friends. She keeps Heather's confidence high by constantly encouraging her.

Lance has been a keeper of mine for eleven years, and has taught me more about wisdom than anyone else. We have fantastic discussions exploring the Kingdom together. He is a warrior.

Tim, who has been in my life for five years, is my
youngest keeping friendship. He is
stunning in his ability to walk with me,
explore the future, and think in areas
I'm not capable of thinking in. He really
cares about me, to the extent that he
sold his house and bought a new one
with a guest house so that I could have a place to stay
when I am in California.

> "As iron sharpens iron, so a
> man sharpens the
> countenance of his friend."
> Proverbs 27:17

there are different levels of keeping relationship

Some keeping relationships are mutual in depth and
significance. Others have varying levels of
reciprocation. We must be led by the Spirit. It is
important that we check out our desires and
motivations before proceeding.

First, learn to receive God as your Keeper. Without
this as our bedrock, our keeping may become too
demanding and unrealistic. Learn to revel in being kept
by God so that you become aware of how to keep
others.

There is only a narrow gap between giving advice
and taking control. Resist the urge to fix your friend's
life. Rather walk with them in it and enable them to
reach their own conclusions. Mostly in relationships we
walk in grace before truth. That is, we hold on to people
as they are trying to "get it". We don't force-feed

answers because people do not grow up in that context. There are times, however, when we need to exercise loving confrontation as we talk about issues more openly.

Keeping is not controlling. It is not dominating people but being there for them, releasing them and supporting their efforts to put on Christ. I am not responsible for how people turn out. I am responsible for my friendship.

The people I am keeping are not controlled by me. They do not have to run everything by me. I am not displeased or angry if I am not consulted. Keeping is about what I am doing for others. They do not need my permission or approval for anything. If something goes wrong and I was not involved in the decision-making process, I would still support as fully as I am able. We help each other learn. We give loving feedback. Keepers ask relevant questions to help our friendships process through mistakes and difficult times. Of course, if these types of incidents persist it would be wise to explore whether your friendships as keeper are really working.

Some keep me financially by supporting the ministry with regular giving. Others send me a flow of encouragement because they sit before the Lord listening. A couple of people oversee the ministry finances. Some guys occupy a valuable place of relaxation in my life. We watch soccer and rugby together, talk about sport, music and movies. We go for

a quiet beer and a game of snooker or pool. They
de-stress my life. I get to just hang out. They keep me
sane, normal and real. We make gentle fun of each
other, tell stories and laugh out loud. Occasionally we
may chat through something spiritual that they may be
facing, where I may have advice or wisdom. I seldom
confide in them as I have other people I can go to for
my own counsel.

Sometimes our keeping is restricted because we have
a wider call on our life. My friendship with Lance is like
that. He has an international ministry. We love hanging
out together. It tends to be strategic, prophetic and
based on our love of the Kingdom. We hang out in
coffee shops, we go to movies and watch TV over at his
house, but we are very aware that our relationship is
strategically spiritual for the most part.

Because a high-level keeping relationship in my life
will certainly involve warfare, it is not appropriate for
me to fully engage with everyone. I am a warrior and
therefore I need people who can relish the fight and
will stand with me in everything.

I enjoy all the varying people who make up the
community of my friends around the world. Define
your relationships and avoid assumptions. At what
level can you initially engage with your friends? All
good friendships are adjustable. You must dialogue
through the next phase of change. Be realistic about
what you cannot do, where you may have no expertise

to cover particular issues. Your friendship here may be 100% general, rather than specific.

Keep talking, keep defining and refining your love. As you do so your own appreciation of the love and keeping power of God will continuously increase. We become to others as God is to us.

conclusion

In Genesis 4:9, God and Cain had a conversation. *"Then the LORD said to Cain, 'Where is Abel your brother?' He said, 'I do not know. Am I my brother's keeper?'"* The answer to that question is a resounding YES! We are called to keep one another as God has kept us.

God longs for us to be wholehearted in our love for Him, and in our love for one another. He does not want us to sit back and withhold ourselves. He longs for us to enter relationships that honor and worship Him. When we live in unity, God can bring us into a deeper existence in the realm of the Spirit.

> "Two are better than one, because they have a good reward for their labor."
> Ecclesiastes 4:9

It is my prayer that Christians would become the family, the company of friends that God desires us to be. If our friendships are continually strengthened and stand the test of time, we will become an enigma in the earth. People will look at us and marvel. 1 John 3:16 says:

*By this we know love, because He laid down His
life for us. And we also ought to lay down our lives
for the brethren.*

Our friendships can make God's heart glad.

We must not back down, break down, or run away,
but instead run together and break through into
everything He has called us to be.

practical relationship building

The following exercises are part of a set of values that I wrote some time ago. They will enable you to bring some definition into the area of your friendships.

In each exercise:

▶ Take the time to read the scriptures several times, first quietly, then out loud.

▶ Study them, especially the key words and concepts.

▶ Meditate on them fully. In particular:
a. This is how the Holy Spirit operates in your life. What does that mean to you?
b. Think about the implications of moving in these values as part of your lifestyle of spirituality.

▶ Allow the statements to flow into your life.

▶ Under the Action headings, take steps to fulfill each point.

▶ Consider your own Value Statements and re-write them to suit your own perceptions and circumstances.

eight exercises

Scriptures
► John 15:9
► Romans 12:10
► Colossians 3:12–17
► 1 Corinthians 13:1–13
► 1 Peter 4:8
► Matthew 5:21–24

Thought Points
There is nothing we can do to make God love us more and there is nothing we can do that would make Him love us less! His love is based on who He is within Himself, not on our performance.

He is consistent and faithful in how He loves us. His love is never on the negotiating table when we are in dispute and disrepute with Him. How can we be anything less for each other?

His love enables us to be true to one another when we have difficulties. Keeping His way of loving in the forefront of our minds in times of complexity helps us to be true to God in the way that we hold on to one another.

- ▶ Love means being patient and expressing kindness.
- ▶ Love does not remember slights, hold grudges or recall bad history.
- ▶ Love is unselfish and thoughtful.
- ▶ Loving people bear all things well and believe the best of others.
- ▶ Truly forgiving and forgetting is the hallmark of God's love in us.
- ▶ Love is not provoked and forgoes vengeance.
- ▶ Love never fails.
- ▶ Be devoted to one another in brotherly love.
- ▶ Love is an action not just a word.
- ▶ Real love allows people to change.

Action

Think of someone recently where you have not fully been the loving person the Holy Spirit was expecting you to be in the situation … and be reconciled.

Take time to thoughtfully upgrade your love with the people around you.

Value Statement

Non-negotiable love is being the best expression of Christ to another human being. Putting love first and last in every situation keeps us in the abiding Presence of God.

Non-negotiable love can heal and seal every problem that may occur in any relationship.

exercise 2: relationships of openness and honesty

Scriptures
- ► Romans 12:9
- ► Ephesians 4:15
- ► Romans 2:1–11
- ► 2 Corinthians 4:1–2
- ► Romans 6:12–14
- ► 2 Corinthians 7:1–2
- ► 1 John 1:5–10

Thought Points
A truly humble person does not fear being exposed. The great weakness in the western church is our refusal to accept that brokenness is a part of all life in the Spirit.

His power works best in weak people. Living in loving accountable relationships together enables us to walk in the light with God and give no place to the enemy.

Self-disclosure is vital to that process. A group of people who each know a part of our life and, together, know it all.

- ► Public and personal integrity through accountable friendships.
- ► It is the secret areas of our life where Jesus is not Lord.
- ► Humility and honesty have the same root.

- ▶ Self-disclosure is a process involving definition.
- ▶ Humble people are:
  - small in their own eyes
  - honest about their struggles
  - open to constructive criticism
- ▶ Trust that you are loved, accepted, forgiven, and redeemed.

Action

To begin the process of self-disclosure and openness, start to look around and discover who, in friendship, may be trusted, over time, with certain parts of your life. Begin to develop a friendship with those people.

It takes time and love expressed and received before we can trust ourselves to self-disclosure. The important thing is having a plan for friendship that includes accountability.

Value Statement

Relationships of openness and honesty allow us to drop the mask and the image we unconsciously present to the world. In this way we live in conscious freedom and joy before people as we do before God. Accepted in the Beloved, accepted in the Body, accepted by self.

exercise 3: believing the best

Scriptures
- 1 Corinthians 13:7 – 8
- Romans 12:10 – 12
- Philippians 4:8
- Titus 1:15
- Colossians 3:12 – 17
- Luke 6:31

Thought Points

How we see people is often a mirror image of how we see ourselves. How we accept others is a significant indicator of our own self-acceptance in Christ. We believe the best about others because we believe the truth about ourselves in Jesus.

Giving others the benefit of the doubt will lessen the doubts we have about ourselves. This enables us to express an incredible depth of love and freedom to people. We are bestowing the gift of acceptance and receiving it afresh in each human transaction.

- Be patient with your, and others', defects.
- Treat others how you would love to be treated.
- Love is the perfect bond of unity.
- Be devoted to one another in love and prefer one another in honor.

- ▶ Do not be wise in your own estimation, be humble.
- ▶ Respect what is right, cover what is wrong in grace.
- ▶ Practice Philippians 4:8!
- ▶ Relational breakdowns are really opportunities for a breakthrough … cunningly disguised!

Action

Ask the Holy Spirit to enable you to see people as He does. Think of how you would speak to them with His new found understanding. Be aware that tense moments in relationships give you special opportunities to practice loving acceptance by believing the best.

Value Statement

It is impossible to grow relationships when living in an atmosphere of disapproval. Believing the best about people is not about ignoring their faults but about recognizing that everyone wants to change and become like Jesus. We are always a work in progress and therefore deserving of mercy, grace and love.

Whenever we see Christ in one another, He is present!

exercise 4: always declare your commitment

Scriptures
- ▶ Philippians 2:1-4
- ▶ Colossians 3:12-17
- ▶ Jude 20, 21
- ▶ Colossians 2:1-7
- ▶ Romans 9:1-5
- ▶ Romans 1:8-15

Thought Points
Every situation (good or bad) is an opportunity to express what the Lord has put in our hearts. Relationships are about promises. Word given and word kept. There is no commitment that is not first spoken and meant.

In football terms, declaring your commitment gets you out of the stands and into the game. It makes you a participant, not an onlooker. The strength of Paul's declared commitment was full of passion (Romans 9:1-5).

In every circumstance, we must declare our positive intention. In times of tension and difficulty, silence can be wounding. Never assume that people know how much you are for them. Always declare it with thoughtfulness and love.

- ▶ Be intentional to one another.
- ▶ Plan to be someone's good friend.

▶ Live out who you really are with people.
▶ Being devoted to people means being committed through good times and bad.
▶ Take time to upgrade your current friendships.
▶ Express affection and compassion.
▶ Maintain the same love even when people are inconsistent.
▶ Declaring your commitment makes a difference to you as well as others.

Action

Meditate on the people around you who mean the most to you. Think about them and what they are facing and declare a commitment to that friendship. A word, a card, a gesture, a gift, a phone call – these little things will make a lot of difference to someone and you will feel better about yourself.

Value Statement

Declaring your commitment to others is the best way of understanding and receiving God's commitment to you. The Bible is God's declaration of commitment to humanity. His whole heart is in His word to us. When you declare your commitment, your heart follows your involvement.

exercise 5: truth wrapped in love, preceded by grace

Scriptures

▶ Ephesians 4:15, 25–27
▶ Hebrews 4:14–16
▶ Colossians 3:12–17
▶ John 1:14–17
▶ Luke 6:36–38
▶ James 2:12–13
▶ Matthew 18:15–20

Thought Points

God is determined that our relationships should be earthed in reality and not fantasy. He is committed to truth and trust, mercy and grace, and loving acceptance.

Speaking the truth in love, understanding the weakness of people and enabling them to become confident in God's mercy and grace, are all great tests of our own maturity in the Lord.

As we give these things they come back to us, pressed down, shaken together and running over.

▶ Mercy triumphs over judgment.
▶ Grace and truth come by Jesus Christ.
▶ Always grace before truth.
▶ Be merciful, just as God is merciful.
▶ Grace humbles us and makes our heart accessible to others.

- ► Humility and compassion are the keys to truth telling.
- ► Pardon and you will be pardoned.
- ► Truth telling releases people to experience God's grace.

Action
Think of an issue you may currently have with an individual.

- ► Pray about them until compassion fills your heart.
- ► Make sure there are no grounds for hypocrisy in you.
- ► Think of the truth you need to express. How should you say it? How would you like it spoken to you? Do likewise!

Value Statement
Truth is not just about being right, but also about doing right. Truth given without compassion and love may destroy someone's world. This is your opportunity to win someone's heart to a greater love in Christ. When acceptance and truth combine with loving kindness, people are made whole.

exercise 6: character before gifting

Scriptures
- ▶ 1 Corinthians 12:4–13:3
- ▶ 1 Timothy 1:12–17
- ▶ Luke 18:9–14
- ▶ Titus 1:15–3:11
- ▶ Galatians 5:22–23
- ▶ 1 Timothy 4:6–16

Thought Points

Christ in you is your only defence against the enemy, carnality and your own vanity. Listen to the righteous assessment of godly people around you. Accept what they can see about you rather than what you cannot see about your own morality.

We all have blind spots about ourselves where we struggle to be faithful. This is when we need the love and support of people who are for us and want us to succeed.

The best way to change is to fasten your attention upon God and godly people and allow both to speak into your life. Do not be overly sensitive to criticism, nor inflated by praise. Instead recognize your brokenness, acknowledge your gifts and refuse to take yourself too seriously.

- ▶ Humble yourself and God will exalt you.

▶ Pay attention to your character flaws ... the
   enemy does!
▶ Gifts are for the common good, so is your
   character.
▶ Membership of the Body depends upon your
   Christ-likeness not your spiritual gifting.
▶ You will destroy with your character what God has
   built with your gift.
▶ Discipline yourself in godliness ... the best form of
   control is self-control.

Action

If you were in court, charged with being righteous,
godly, and an example of good character, what would
be the evidence that would convict you? Meditate on
that and do what seems good to the Holy Spirit.

Value Statement

Not valuing character will diminish your gift. When
your progress in godliness is visible, your
trustworthiness will increase and your anointing will
expand.

exercise 7: give and it shall be given

Scriptures

- ▶ 1 Thessalonians 5:18
- ▶ 2 Peter 1:2–15
- ▶ Ephesians 3:14–21
- ▶ 2 Corinthians 9:6–15
- ▶ 1 Peter 4:9
- ▶ Romans 12:13
- ▶ Luke 6:30–38
- ▶ Acts 20:32–35

Thought Points

Giving is not just about finances or ministry. It is also about bestowing life, love and laughter into the lifestyles of others. It is about having a generous nature with all that God has given us.

Whatever God gives must be multiplied in us. God does not intend lack or reduction, so your willingness to sow is a major clue to your ability to receive. His generosity, graciousness and extravagance teaches us to pray with outrageous confidence. He has a capacity to release beyond our ability to conceive or request.

There is usually a subtle and elegant test that surrounds our giving to the Lord. He will make a request for increase just as our resources (human and financial) are dwindling and we are feeling the pinch.

Faithfulness is critical to the life-style of generosity that God has called us to walk with Him.

- ▶ God is your provision, not your resource.
- ▶ Give "such as you have" (love, peace, friendship...)
- ▶ The spirit behind your giving means more to God than the gift you release.
- ▶ It is better to give than to receive.
- ▶ You cannot plant and harvest on the same day, so always plan your giving in advance of your need.

Action
Whatever you need, be the first to give it!

Value Statement
If God can pass it through you, He will give it to you.

exercise 8: stewardship not ownership

Scriptures
- ▶ 1 Peter 4:10–11
- ▶ Romans 15:1–7
- ▶ 1 Corinthians 10:24, 33
- ▶ Philippians 2:1–18
- ▶ 2 Corinthians 12:14–18
- ▶ Luke 16:10–13
- ▶ 1 Corinthians 4:2

Thought Points
Stewardship is a lifestyle. It is not just about ministry. Our life and the way we choose to live it is our reasonable worship and service to the Lord. We must recapture a sense of stewardship for our relationships: family and friends, our time, conversations, our job, and our place in the body of Christ.

Many Christians give God a part (tithe) of their lives in church attendance (meetings), but are fully in control of the rest of their time themselves. We own our lives rather than living them in extended stewardship above the Christian norm. Jesus must be Lord over everything and every part of our life must feel His redemptive and loving touch.

He is a faithful steward over our lives and it is fitting that our stewardship towards Him, be just as intentional.

▶ Fix your heart and mind on stewardship.

▶ Be a steward of the manifold grace of God.

▶ Our stewardship is always for the benefit of others.

▶ Ownership causes strife, stewardship produces rest and peace.

▶ Even Jesus did not please Himself.

▶ Glorifying God is a steward's main motivation.

▶ He who is faithful in small things will be trusted with much.

Action

Write your own obituary!

Imagine that when you have passed on to be with the Father, a Christian magazine wanted to write an article on your life as an example of good stewardship. What would you want the main points to say?

Identifying these main points will give us something definite to aim for so that we can become as intentional as the Father.

Value Statement

Stewardship is the intentional pursuit of God to involve Him in everything – the Holy Spirit ruling your life with your full co-operation.

consider this . . .

▶ What is the one thing about God that you love the most?

▶ What is the one aspect of God's nature that you need the most in your current circumstances?

NB The answer to both these questions will tell you:

▶ What the Holy Spirit is teaching you about the Father.

▶ What the Spirit is building into your own life and character at this time.

friendships ... friendships

Think of people around your life who are significant for you and for whom you have deep affection.

1. Name them!
2. How can you upgrade your love and commitment to each person?
3. What specific support do each of your friends most need now? How do you plan to be that for them?
4. What particular encouragement can you bring to each of these relationships?
5. Whom do you want as your own keeper?
   - Do you want them as general overall keeping relationship to support you in every circumstance?
   - Is there a specific area in your life where you can make a request for them to keep you?
6. Are there people whom you feel a call to act as a keeper?
   - Do you wish to be an overall keeper for them to offer support in every situation?
   - Is there a specific area in their life where you can be of particular benefit to them?

7. The people you nominate in (5) may be different from those you identify in (6). That is fine. Remember that definition is absolutely essential.
   – What dialogue will you enter into with each person?

extra exercise: lectio divina

Lectio Divina (Latin for *divine reading*) is an ancient way of reading the Bible – allowing a quiet and contemplative way of coming to God's Word. Lectio Divina opens the pulse of the Scripture, helping readers dig far deeper into the Word than normally happens in a quick glance-over.

In this exercise, we will look at a portion of Scripture and use a modified Lectio Divina technique to engage it. This technique can be used on any piece of Scripture; I highly recommend using it for key Bible passages that the Lord has highlighted for you, and for anything you think might be an inheritance word for your life (see the *Crafted Prayer interactive journal* for more on inheritance words).

Though I speak with the tongues of men and of angels, but have not love, I have become sounding brass or a clanging cymbal. And though I have the gift of prophecy, and understand all mysteries and all knowledge, and though I have all faith, so that I could remove mountains, but have not love, I am nothing. And though I bestow all my goods to feed the poor, and though I give my body to be burned, but have not love, it profits me nothing.

Love suffers long and is kind; love does not envy; love does not parade itself, is not puffed up; does not behave rudely, does not seek its own, is not provoked, thinks no evil; does not rejoice in iniquity, but rejoices in the truth; bears all things, believes all things, hopes all things, endures all things.

Love never fails. But whether there are prophecies, they will fail; whether there are tongues, they will cease; whether there is knowledge, it will vanish away. For we know in part and we prophesy in part. But when that which is perfect has come, then that which is in part will be done away.

When I was a child, I spoke as a child, I understood as a child, I thought as a child; but when I became a man, I put away childish things. For now we see in a mirror, dimly, but then face to face. Now I know in part, but then I shall know just as I also am known.

And now abide faith, hope, love, these three; but the greatest of these is love. (1 Corinthians 13)

1. Find a place of stillness before God. Embrace His peace. Calm your body, breathe slowly ... clear your mind of the distractions of life. Ask God to reveal His rest to you. Whisper the word, "Stillness." This can take some time, but once you're in that place of rest, enjoy it. Worship God out of it.

2. Read the passage twice, slowly.

   a. Allow its words to become familiar to you, and sink into your spirit. Picture Paul writing this chapter – become part of it. Listen for pieces that catch your attention.

b. Following the reading, meditate upon what you have heard. What stands out? Write it down:

. . . .
. . . .
. . . .
. . . .

c. If a word or phrase from the passage seems highlighted to you, write it down:

. . . .
. . . .
. . . .
. . . .

3. Read the passage twice, again.

a. Like waves crashing onto a shore, let the words of the Scripture crash onto your spirit? What are you discerning? What are you hearing? What are you feeling? Write it down:

. . . .
. . . .
. . . .
. . . .

b. What is the theme of this passage? Write it down:

. . . .
. . . .
. . . .
. . . .

c. Does this passage rekindle any memories or experiences? Write it down:

. . . .
. . . .
. . . .
. . . .

d. What is the Holy Spirit saying to you? Write it down:

. . . .
. . . .
. . . .
. . . .

4. Read the passage two final times.
   a. Meditate on it.
   b. Is there something God wants you to do with this passage? Is there something He is calling you to? Write it down:

. . . .
. . . .
. . . .
. . . .

   c. Pray silently. Tell God what this Scripture is leading you to think about. Ask Him for His thoughts. Write down your conversation – as if you and God are sitting in a coffee shop, two old and dear friends, sharing:

. . . .
. . . .

5. Pray and thank God for what He has shared with you. Come back to the passage a few more times over the coming weeks.

FAQ:

frequently asked questions

Q. *Who is Graham Cooke and how can I find more information about him?*

A. Graham is a speaker and author who lives in Vacaville, California. He has been involved in prophetic ministry since 1974. He has developed a series of training programs on prophecy; leadership; spirituality; devotional life; walking in the Spirit; and spiritual warfare. All of which have received international acclaim for their depth of insight, revelation and wisdom.

Graham serves on the leadership team of The Mission in Vacaville where he is part of a think tank exploring the future and developing strategies for onward momentum and progression.

You can learn more about Graham at www.grahamcooke.com.

Q. *How can I become a prayer partner with Graham?*

A. Check his website, www.grahamcooke.com, for all of the information you need.

Q. *Has Graham written any other books?*

A. To date Graham has written 4 books; co-authored 1 more and written 8 Interactive Journals. These are:

Books:

- ➢ Developing Your Prophetic Gifting (now out of print).
- ➢ A Divine Confrontation ... Birth Pangs of the New Church.
- ➢ Approaching the Heart of Prophecy [Volume 1, Prophetic Series].
- ➢ Prophecy & Responsibility [Volume 2, Prophetic Series].

Journals:

- ➢ Hiddenness & Manifestation [Book 1, Being with God Series].
- ➢ Crafted Prayer [Book 2, Being with God Series].
- ➢ The Nature of God [Book 3, Being with God Series].
- ➢ Beholding and Becoming [Book 4, Being with God Series].
- ➢ Towards a Powerful Inner Life [Book 5, Being with God Series].

- ➢ The Language of Promise [Book 6, Being with God Series].
- ➢ Living in Dependency and Wonder [Book 7, Being with God Series].
- ➢ God's Keeping Power [Book 8, Being with God Series].
- ➢ Qualities of a Spiritual Warrior [Volume 1, The Way of the Warrior Series].

<u>Co-author:</u>
- ➢ Permission Granted with Gary Goodell

All are available at www.brilliantbookhouse.com.

About the Author

Graham Cooke is part of The Mission core leadership team, working with senior team leader, David Crone, in Vacaville, California. Graham's role includes training, consulting, mentoring, and being part of a think tank to examine the journey from present to future.

He is married to Theresa who has a passion for worship and dance. She loves to be involved in intercession, warfare, and setting people free. She cares about injustice, abuse, and has compassion on people who are sick, suffering, and disenfranchised.

They have six children and one grandchild. Ben and Seth [32 and 30] both reside and work in the UK. Ben is developing as a writer, is very funny, and probably knows every movie ever made. Seth is a musician, a deep thinker with a caring outlook and amazing capacity for mischief.

Sophie, and son-in-law Mark, live in Vacaville and attend The Mission. Sophie is the Pastoral Assistant for The Mission and Graham's ministry FTI. Sophie has played a significant part in Graham's ministry for a number of years, and has helped develop resources, new books and journals, as well as organize events. Mark and Sophie are a warm-hearted, friendly, deeply humorous couple with lots of friends. Their daughter, Evelyn (August 2006) is a delight — a happy little soul who likes music, loves to dance, and enjoys books.

Daughters Alexis and Alyssa live in Sacramento. Alexis is loving, kind, and gentle. She is very intuitive and steadfast toward her friends. Alyssa is a very focused and determined young woman who is fun loving with a witty sense of humor.

Also, Graham and Theresa have two beautiful young women, Julianne and Megan, both in Australia, who are a part of their extended family.

Graham is a popular conference speaker and is well known for his training programs on the prophetic, spiritual warfare, intimacy and devotional life, leadership, spirituality, and the church in transition. He functions as a consultant and free thinker to businesses, churches, and organizations, enabling them to develop strategically. He has a passion to establish the Kingdom and build prototype churches that can fully reach a post-modern society.

A strong part of Graham's ministry is in producing finances and resources to the poor and disenfranchised in developing countries. He supports many projects specifically for widows, orphans, and people in the penal system. He hates abuse of women and works actively against human trafficking and the sex slave trade, including women caught up in prostitution and pornography.

If you would like to invite Graham to minister at an event, please complete our online Ministry Invitation Form at www.grahamcooke.com.

If you wish to become a financial partner for the sake of missions and compassionate acts across the nations, please contact his office at <u>office@grahamcooke.com</u> where his personal assistant, Jeanne Thompson, will be happy to assist you.

Graham has many prayer partners who play a significant part in supporting his ministry through intercession and sponsorship. Prayer partners have the honor to be Graham's shield. They are his defensive covering that allows him to advance the Kingdom all over the world. The partners are a vital part of Graham's interdependent team. If you are interested in becoming a prayer partner, please contact his international coordinator, Pam Jarvis, at <u>prayer@grahamcooke.com</u>.

You may contact Graham by writing to:

Graham Cooke
6391 Leisure Town Road
Vacaville, California
USA 95687
<u>www.grahamcooke.com</u>